Kent

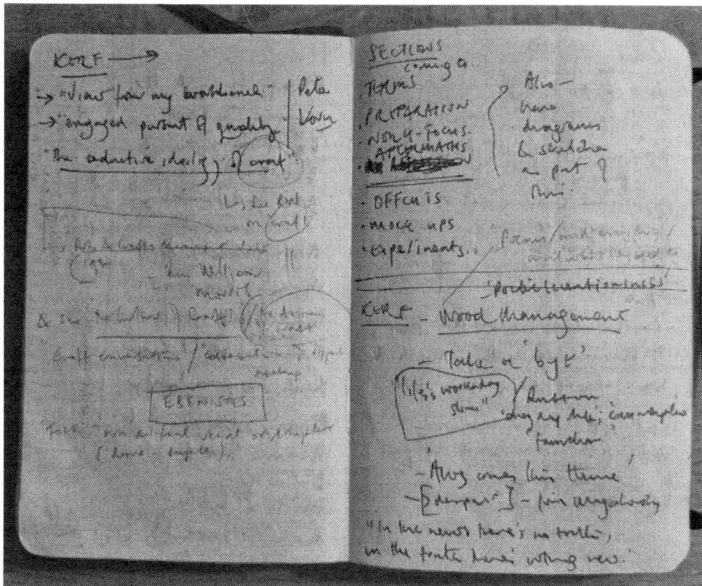

Gareth Farmer

Published 2022 by the87press

The 87 Press LTD

87 Stonecot Hill

Sutton

Surrey

SM3 9HJ

www.the87press.co.uk

ISBN: 978-1-7399547-7-2

Design: Stanislava Stoilova [www.sdesign.graphics]

For Alice Barnaby, Mandy Bloomfield, Peter Middleton,
Ben Pitcher and Tim Shortis.
Always an apprentice in the ateliers of your teachings.

Contents

Kerf. A Brief Excursus

Kerf (kə:f) [OE. *cyrf* (ME. *kirf, kerf*):- Gmc. **kurbiz,* f. **kurb- *kerb-* CARVE; cf. ON. *kurfr* chip, *kyrfa* cut, and ME., mod. dial. CARF.] **1.** The act of cutting; a cut, stroke; power of cutting. Now *rare*. **2.** The incision made by cutting, esp. by a saw 1523. **3.** The cut end or surface on a tree or branch ME. **4.** A cutting (of anything) 1678.

Referring to etymologies offers a performance of authenticity and rootedness; I'm keen on such pretentions. The Old English origin of the word 'kerf' is pleasing: *cyrf*, like putting an ornately camp curse on someone. The voicing is pleasurable: from the throat-back guttural tenuis, through to the gentle explosion of the labio-dental spirant. *Kerf.* The word refers, simply, to the hole created in wood by a saw blade. The size of the kerf depends on the size, width, or 'set', of the saw blade. With a sharp and accurate blade, a 2/8-inch cut will create the equivalent hole in the wood. Knowing one's kerf, as no one says, is like knowing one's worth. It is important to account for kerf when measuring and cutting wood, as such offcuts aren't coming back. Cutting a two-by-four in half is, in fact, cutting two separate pieces with the middle kerf cut absent. If you want to measure and build accurately, you need to know how much of the wood your saw blade is taking out.

I discovered the word in the last few years. It was described, accurately, by one youtuber as an 'essential' word to know if one is to become a proficient woodworker. I am becoming a proficient woodworker but, as I am also a writer, part of the mastery of this craft for me requires learning the specialist vocabulary of this field. *router, awl, shakes, chamfer.* (See the Glossary for some delights). My developing interest in woodwork was enabled by a fortuitous move to a small cottage in central Bedfordshire, whose garden happened to possess a small, brick and already-electrified outhouse. This is now the workshop – or *atelier* – of GSF Woodwork (find them on Instagram and Etsy!). My woodwork journey began making some crudely designed, poorly constructed and slightly wonky shelves for my study. Over time, I have become a little better with every build, aided by many books on woodworking techniques, tips and tricks, ample hours spent envying workshops on the youtubes, and many, many, many days of error and trial.

Why am I writing this? Well, 'kerf' is not only a practical concept for application, but a concept enabling abstractions about the practical. Kerf are the detritus, the excess, the rejected parts of wood, never to be regained and usually forgotten about after extraction. Kerf is the ever-amassing silent abject of any wood project. To recklessly allegoricalise the word, we might, I thought, consider other instances of 'kerf' in our everyday worlds; in other words, kerf might be a useful, if clunky, metaphor for many rejected, marginalised or essential-but-disposal things and people. We might, for example, think about people, processes and institutions who are treated as, or who produce, 'kerf' in society and culture. Such people could be those with disabilities, minority or minoritised people and cultures, as well as the labour processes and exploitations under capitalism. Interesting. But the triteness of the metaphor itched. I may not be able to write clearly about any of these things without reducing them to the status of a worthily performative poetics; art for tart's sate. I don't want to do that.

The poems of *Kerf* do feature veiled veins of the above ideas, but its abiding themes are probably: woodworking, craft, labour, autism and, in particular, the unique languages and language practices of each of these non-discreet areas of activity. A reader may put these themes in their backpack to extract and chew on as they journey through this book. But two points of interest about this author might also be of relevance: he is a neophyte woodworker, as we now know, and he was diagnosed with Autistic Spectrum Disorder (ASD or, in old money, Asperger Syndrome) at the age of forty. While all the poems overtly hint and covertly glimpse these things, the last, long poem sequence, 'What's That: Instead of Ego', attempts to write about three things at once: the planning and execution of a non-specific woodwork project; woodworking and craft in general, and the strange process of being diagnosed with ASD.

It might not be a coincidence that I have found solace in the solitary wordlessness of woodworking. It is a labour process to which I can entirely give myself for hours and days, with only mumbles, grunts and repeated and un-audited stims to accompany me. I like the repetition, order and logic of woodwork. I also like retreating from the responsibilities of performing social interactions with boring language, avoiding having to constrain my mind to complete administrative tasks, and having a break from the exhausting but unwilling assemblage of verbal and interactive hyper-data from all the other aspects of my everyday. I like the slow processes and processing of taming wood. I also prefer the company of tools to many other interactions; they're logical, obvious and won't confuse me. A separate part of my intellectual engagement with woodwork features analysis of labour and craft and their relationships with the co-production of writing. But that's for another day and that, for now, is that about my life.

I don't want to be disingenuous, but I also do not want not to be ingeniously disengaged either. There is autobiography here seeded, though its emergence in shoots and buds is erratic and restrained by evasive and hostile soils. Why? I've read dozens of wonderful and intriguing autistic memoirs by brilliant people and I don't think I can yet write with the lucidity, confidence or grace that these possess. Also, this is poetry: the seat of mannered evasion; the mode of methodological metonymy. Directness is for the lingua-frankly and, frankly, I'm no good at it. That being stated: the 'he' and 'I' throughout may well betray accidental missteps of Gareth Farmer stumbling into semi-transparency, glimpsed before the reactive reassurances of opacity consume grammatical cogency. There may be no history of cynical realisation that is not, also, the twistery of complicit animadversion. Such a sentiment is sedimented in every line of this book.

But. But. Maybe this book does join the ranks of quirkle-perkery. In which case: *Hi, peeps!*

Sincerely though: with thanks to anyone who takes the time to read this book. I am grateful.

Enjoy.

Gareth Farmer
Shefford, 2nd April 2022.

Anne Boldet —

(i) "Pedantic" / Professorial

(ii) Use pt. of Artistic Disturbances
& create poem out of
word ... incorporate
1 word per line.

& *(ii)* Poem using any
diagram papers

(iii) heuristics — about "rules"
and sentences

(iv) Mnemonics & CARRIAGE
→ one G off — on Eupers

PLANS:
× "Sensoria"
× Pedeath — what?
× Vet — tumor
○ "roundtable" on Small Poems
a "CAMPUS"
⊙ TB11 — Neurodivergence politics
③ Dahlia =   (×) Out of   "the
                                  order   pitcher
                                  is out."
(v) hefts person ship
     — of one Suicide & reflect
     on drawing dance

(vii) HR poem (using print out)
(viii) Oliver Sacks The Mind Travellers
                      series.
(ix) System Architecture & totalitarian
                      thinking =

Cognitive Loading

Try working backwards, from vision to enabling.
Rules will, efficiently, inculcate as apparent roots.
It's a cognitive stylisation and anti-optimal, where
Approximations become neonatal satisfaction solutions.
Loose bounds for a rationality outflanking algorithm.
Abstractions are autisticised, operating out of formal bonds.
Never to be understood beyond the iterations in glimpses.
Dead-ringer through identi-kitting the blasé balance of poise.
Efficiency models of attributable experiential grids are
Re-routed through predictable tests of deficiency and desire.
Requiring local calculations, these modulations mimic progress.
Options for availability-logic or anchored-expectation are
        erroneous.
"Rare it is to see" social proof that stands up to reason.
Recognise in others the baselines by which to rhythm-boogie;
Understood as 'The Popular': the grids by which to portion
        passion.
Landmarks of cultural proprioception anchor the cognitive load;
Ecological orientation within minimised inaccuracy and risk.
Oh! To know the way to happiness, that rationality to
        critique-park.
For all else, produce a survey: "What, to you, is contentment?"
Take buffet tables and their etiquettes. Buffetiquettes:
Hazard-reducing the seductions of finger-suck; conveyor
        comportment;
Unfurl the unconfirmed rumour about bacterial growth regimes;
Make bounded efforts not to cross-contaminate crabby
        efficiency rules.
Be appropriate. It is never appropriate to fondle vol-au-vents.
        Ever.
Educational backgrounds are musts for the hierarchical
        heuristics,

Decision-quickeners for greater accuracy of class contagion
and mirror co-aid-gent-see.

Unbelievably, the knowing nod enables entrance. Must've
been the tome-tuck.

Called out at every High Table awkwardness and Hegel-less
small talk.

Affect is a misnomer, unless rebarbative in Spinoza-spin and
served as such.

Taste is another marker, itemised in the retro of classical
cassette racks.

Escalation of commitment uniforms-up when challenged.

Default to other cheek-*tourne*, willed into abjection by
objectionable ordinances.

Gestalts are naturalised as quick-think metaphors of progress,

Untethered to the phrases that birthed them and rapidly
reassuring,

Erroneously vulnerable, but adaptive in always seismic
circle-jerk.

Severing with sanction those over-exposed by heuristic refusal
and defiance.

Scope neglect is not anomalous; it's a peak-end rule, socialised.

Intergenerational justice:

mahagony & tweed

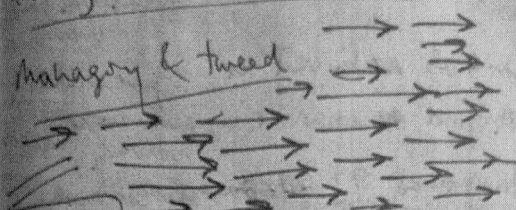

KORE:

every moment edged
lurch drama, ~~every~~ ~~moment~~
unsettle in unstable instabilities
the wait ~~it to~~ for unsettle unsettles
discomfort, discomfit, disconsolate
— a sense of dis'es distinctive ~~every day~~
every day
with fragility, the hope for future
community
with ~~the~~ adjacent moments of hope
~~without~~ the ~~worth~~ of 'whether' worrying
and wearing at the elbow grease of attempted
ease
tweedy memories and aspirations
fail a fulcrum
by
~~which to~~ leave & heaven hard-
wembed a volume ~~~~

Overshare

Does he? News bulletins were never so prescribed.
Control the story by half-strategic vulnerability.
At ease, appease, release as open wounds,
The want to claim want with affront of info.
Do I? Is not this detailed excurses,
The modality of minutely 'laid bare',
The route and routine of conviviality?

> *"You'll have a nice off,"* she sneered.
> *"You're always insincere,"* he withered.

Confusion etched in protuberances of perseveration.
Circumambulation to ambulate towards connection.
Cackled and babbled badinage is permissible;
Compassion-fuelled contextualisation is inadmissible.
The 'open wounds' are preposterously porous –
Particularly when scarified within quotation marks –
After ponderous pedantry on answer's aetiology.
Too much info. to spew, to eschew, a truth.
Too many guardian modes and codes
Secreted in cryptic manuals;
Sequestered as chat intangibles.

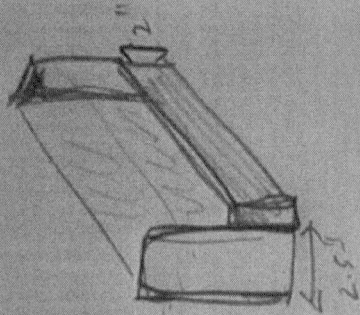

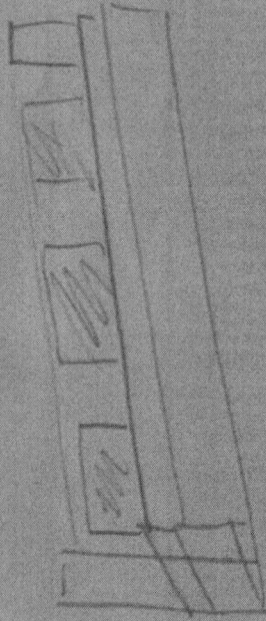

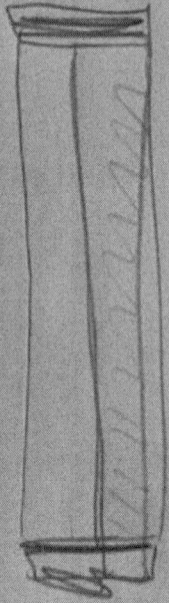

...ine Box +

...t angle w/ knife
...e dent with chisel.
...ak line on width
...o fingers right up against it

...ndpaper Shelves

And, Now What?
for Callie Gardner

"And, now what?"

After the necessity of narrow focus shifts broad-ways?
After the mania of making distracts the ugly,
Alienating abstracts from their keen edges?
Dulled thoughts are back-benched with fumbled hours,
Hunched and hefted through precision making.
Never precise enough, of course, despite kerf-calculations:
The striated chaos of fibres strewn after cut's explanation;
Always more in dust, as in, *in*-expert exploration
Of labour pains, scuffed in knuckles bared and beaten.

"And, now what?"

Through inception-sketches, measure-moments,
Mouthed and mumbled rehearsals of semblance,
Fine and fertile in the febrile conversation of image,
Converted, here, as *inad*-equation of imago-shade.
Through wood choice, scratch, scrape and scramble
To obtain, purloin, beg and hollow-out to assemble.
Through saw and sand. Eager to fondle the finished
Boards, to ache and harry a finish, a once-again feeble
Furnishment of a projected constellation of hope.

"And, now what?"

After ideas become arranged in the *#actuallyactual*,
The derangement of the manic distraction jointing?
Relief now, dowelled to the tapered hole of "now-forward",
Sequestered in the wonk of the failed conceal of a pocket-hole,
Hinged to the hegemony of idealisms of simplicity,

Malleted in tortuous extension of a metaphoric lexis of craft,
Stretching grotesquely into the work-less woke:
To know no more momentum to keen with sustain
A temporary refrain from presentiments of pain.

day's task to anti-dwell mutates mesmerically
in jumbled wood wastes and scarred in several tasks
the itch to pitch ideas from imagined other lives
folds into a design for a folding table
improv. reigns, fretted through disturbed nights,
desperate to sequester in brick-and-mortar solace
dialectical (*as if*) against noises, mumbles, wash-and-hang-full
the tropics are monologic, which is why pain
forget that looks are up, to sup, to enter the obligations
of functional inhabitation of environments and contexts
mistakes are high stakes: lavishly loathsome left-overs
bile whiling with the acid indigestion of too much othering
and, by 'othering', he means beer, which is not a joke,
but a type of hypo-honesty, de-checked from the defaults
of the projections of wine and 'noble time', anecdotalising
beer & austere and the sheer of concentration
table-top vices are the dull twins, pitched to ransom,
the hangovers of concentrating on distraction
folding hinges await, elatedly anticipated in clothes-line shapes,
intensely designed on the shy and sly, but with verve
despite the cat's cries, the varnish hasn't dried
before all assembles, defunct I-holes mire
argumentatively, after work, signs of distaste emerge
(*pace* noble): the underwriting misery cheque
never to settle by the critical examination of presents
mindful not of the mine-field of mind-less-ness
tearing from labour time the time to mind,
the reclaimed sanctions of unearned mine
the fractionated functionality so simple when
un-exorcised in the oblong pursuit of self
through the life-long regime of relativisation:
songbirds revisit the levitating meal-bugs
hitherto unobtainable, despite feeder fudge,
a spider has webbed these hard corpses

and they wobble plump, enticingly
I'm reminded   NO   a reminder of the chaos
of clean-up; disagreeable disorder needing fix
such is loneliness; such is loneliness; such is loneliness
such is loneliness; such is loneliness; such is loneliness
someone simpler interpellates through the back pause
contra-frivolous privilege auditor ever set to worry
happy the man, and happy he full-known
who, by dull sophistry, can call the pain a boon
mindfully, he reaches through body-hate to feed
the cat
whose glances and gapes are guilt-tipped
plates pile; washing riles; bills smile;
poems servile to the trick of the performative parallel
riffled through sound plan, like the discarded
sawdust of what is now hailed and harked as word-work

'Austin Kleon –
"Keep Going"'

gauche   awkward

Messy [____]

messy
       sympatico   corrupt   solution
                    resolution
              messy ruptures
                            resentment
ambiguous system
    symbiosis   temporary
              item   argan
deceptive   deceitful   yan
                            any
            antics
messy   tics   the blurton
time   systematic
            ticklish
mental   hectic   shyster
imagined   ambivalent stereotype

            Changeable

Almost, but Inquiet at Names

Is it better to follow the ache of possibility, being an *atelier*
    invented state?
The ever-so-slightly manic for usage. Never uncommon to
    fail in the hope
To achieve the actuality as all's project, all's projection;
    rejection-injection.
Having-, being in ownership of-, or possessing a self: ruses
    designed for mug-sides.
It's delusion, though, in its presence; the sup to know nearly.
As days and weeks are splintered around some sort of contact,
There is vying never for a word, with absence as fonder-
    fountains.
I load up the nonsense of longing, serving up perseveration
    and doubt.
It's doubtful he'll ever arrive after the torturous journey over
    the Alps.
And it's all about self-gratification; insomnious erosion and
    inner-mind theory.
Miasma is its *modus obscurandi*, funnelled through tinctures
    of hope.
By limerence, he knelt and wept, wielding an excuse-card,
    well-worn.
Everyday yields anew, a new nuisance and thoughts by which
    to ponder you.
Regions of sense are convoluted into a landmass locked by
    oceanic wave-norms.
Her human forms and faculties are all negligées of name-poems,
Ever itemised as edict-evincers of self-knowledge; roads to
    San Narcisso.
Nestling always near is the sincere attribution of simulacrumbs,
    or the
Codes by which to busy anxious actions into an aetiology of like.

Haughtily rejected on the 'morrow as monotonous
   predictability-*byts*.
Learnéd not by time's lessons, lean into lamentation of a
   new name,
Which anchors each evening with its heavily-hedonic heft
   and pity.
Ur-you, *ur*-her, *ur*-irksome quagmire of not-knowing how
   to speak to it.
Rude it is to read it all as really rather ridiculous or
   ridiculing of the Real.
Absolved by resolve and retroactive re-jig, you rebound
   robustly,
Mentioning not the secret selves which code the catalogue
   of instincts.
It is enervating, as they are, to the ennoblement of each new
   prospect.
Ask-loop via those codicils known as home-spun-wisdom:
Does this *this* look like last time, or does this *this* look like
   lasting?

mud's leg. —

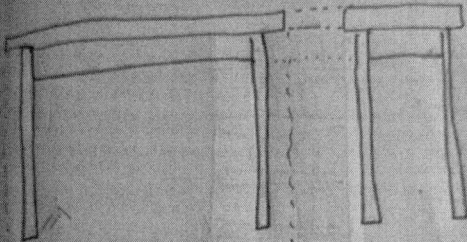

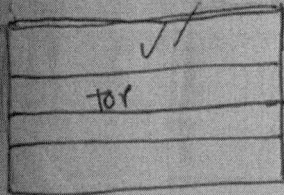

top

underside :—

m & t
joint

apron

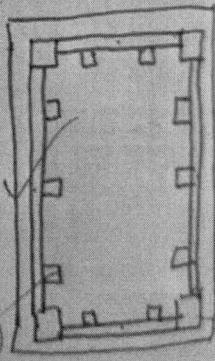

(Biners)

off

To Lock & To Hang

Blind-sided by the solemnity-inducing sanction of probabilities,
We install a lock and measure up for the levelled mirage.
In the gasps between inter-essence, the not-quite-but-almosts,
And with shrinking mentalities in-set to set self-squared all
    'round,
Plans are made. Without fuss, the fiddle to chisel an
    unremarkable female
Through cheapo cardboard pseudo wood, the nestle to
    thrust the interdict.
On questions of aesthetics and will, he is roundly ambiguous
    when questioned,
Tossing self-disappointments as excuses; "whatevering" in
    everything but word.
–submerged semaphores of faux familiarity feign a sense-grasp–
The easy feat is not to mean, as subtle adaptations to the
    faulty, blunt tools
Non-*metier* in the wonk-un-savvy. Strangely malleable
    materials are abject;
Trying to navigate the lightweight and function of new
    surroundings.
A resounding done, here, is far from the feeling of
    accomplishment,
That sensation that one might half imagine as something
    non-analysed.
The wither of the non-thanks is othering, as we turn to the
    mirage-hang.
A semi-ignorant male chorus have proffered profound
    unhelp prior,
And advice prickles like a briar, thorns worn as self-effacing
    penance.
Being in the gloam and gloom of such self-loathing is enervating,
As is witnessing the stooped stance in sustained subordination.

Every second sacrificed to the emotional labour of patience-
    trying stasis.
Deferred to abstract codes, solid-fed over years of
    suppurating superficiality.
Non-said or uttered as each tool fails in finding grasp:

  - wilting and twisting measuring tape, wincing away from
    the clasp
  - snapped pencil led, blunting with impatient impertinence
  - wonky and trust-rusting level
  - bowed, blunted and barely-charged,
    a drill bit dropping in chuck-spin

The despair is not optimistic, or a gift of possibility. It's just
    gruelling.
After the constellation of clashing, contradictory and clawing
    instructions,
Finally settle on a suitably simple methodology (a fragile,
    hour-old offering).
It's tenuous to be in such radical openness in just getting on
    with it.
Measures are in both inches and centimetres; just managing
    avoidance
Of the mutual self-aberration-berration of competitive mind
    maths.
The imperialism of self-rage becomes the metric of self-meaning.
We wobbled the frame up together, a fragile stability of
    commonality,
Stabilised with hard-core screw mawing. Brief relief realised.
    Before.
A wonk is noticed, and the relief unravelled in fractured fission.
The sharpest of Stanley™ knives, that used for placement of
    sending blade,
Could have cut this foggy peasouper, the web-stricken sensibilities

Stuffed into the sentiments made massive by being unspoken.
Without one knowing it: we're having a frayed-off. It's just
agonising.

Addenda
Injunction Grids

strike out
that which
strike out
that which
strikes out
that which

---

bitter self pity
simple in complicity
wither vision of
self as insistent
imposition of unwanted
disposition is haunted

---

petulant impotence
unpleasant unimportance
torpid timidity
prescient divorce
critical call-back
potent petulance

LIMERANCE

- mental state of profound romantic infatuation, deep obsession & continual longing / involuntary state of intense desire.

Atelier -

- artists' or designers studio or workroom

Initialisation or Acronym

* Acronym = new word
* Initialism = just the letters

LOL, e.g. an initialism (laugh out loud) that has become an acronym.

Contra Expressivities

= abrupt shifts in moods and temperament are loss-leaders, intubated = the in-bred self-efface becomes a theoretically visceral reaction to the absent I = your absence is abhorrently infertile to sharing life moments and happy-hefts = as was the learned abstruseness set to furrow almost at friends' brows and adult precocious sayers = you dilated *ad nauseum* about Donne whose fun was underrated in this class = until the adept astuteness of English teachers enabled brief furloughs = learning that aphorisms are heuristics was a voice-drop moment, a single armpit hair *anagnorisis* = delighting in the arbitrary ways in which humans attach meaning to patterned phraseology = out of the magic of Marlowe developed that vocabulary to extend, when you knew it's a fraud = the bareness of others' intuitions became the workshop of note-taking and rote-learning = as the circular logics of language-games were distressed and re-worked, wonky with purpose = watching the wagon wheels wheel & wheel & wheel & wheel and degrammaticalise their drag = you mistake myth-making and mechanical appraisal for creativity and curiousness = there is also a mystique miasma around despair: it's something too old for your apperception = like: who despairs at the disinterment of dictatorial dialogic of the every-day? = is it strange to point to the eccentricities of tables manners and modes of politeness? you ask, curiously = or to delight in silent echolalia of teachers and preachers and leachers whose grammar offends? = the horrors of the five syllables of *ej-ac-ul-a-tion* prevented its mimological achievement = for every other interaction there was the empty space where apparent empathy resided = at least before an understanding about how erratic definitions are in their unsolicited remarks = the tactics of evasion become complex and sketched, rationalised as "down" time = let others exclaim or complain or remain the absorbers of such freak-penance = the swoosh lines of apparent order and cleanliness were wonky. Rather the fractured and fragmented demensions (*sic*) = better to pin one's futility to the in-utility of beauty, rather than the appearance of such = and through the fragments find these hermetic incidents of order, like the geometric relations of hand-gestures = or the fixation on the entropic seep from the hermeticism of codes of conduct between family units: pondered too long = hiding from hiding became a hiding to nothing, as did uber-rationalised entrapments to solution = reveal an idiosyncrasy like, sensitivity, and the Bristol Sharks scrimmage down, calling out M&S skates = crippled by emotion means an inflexible grasp of others' responsibilities and how they are spoiled = an explanation of special circumstance is far from permissible, particularly to popularly traded psychology = these essays on *labyrinthine vestiges of the ethereal* are laughable, but probably not as laughable as the blood-let of allowing ridicule = but having a large vocabulary doth not maketh a fully-understood appearance of simply being in language = diminutives about 'little', 'spite' or 'speciality' are euphemistic; anti-professorships for him, and condemnation to perpetual junior = adulting means interaction with neither the young nor the old – liminal liaisons – and being ridiculed for down-voicing to sophisticated interaction = culture-degree-zero is the highest echelon school friends regard, the ability to be unearthly zero = listing, like this, is the only mode of making without melancholy meltdowns = literally, straight, seriously: list-making is all I do. straight up = sense has always been the least coherence at local levels, whether through seme-weight or rhyme = if the pain cramps of carpel tunnel or the real vamps of hardy fumbles didn't stop, it'd be logorrhoea = the mechanical means by which to reproduce this stuff is simply a laborious lament through language = always more berated for the sedulous blindness to metaphor or colour: can't think thus = but being adept at verbal and scribal mimicry has only seemed a witty deflection from attention = which is why modernism is mainlined on operational mode, contra language and art = to monologue with the High self at the expense of confronting profile, becoming others' messy ways = for all it's worth, it might as well be muting or 'what's that': he's not aged well; not worthy = asking for a moratorium on the fatigued use of 'narrative' to stand in the stead of gaps in reading = as well as lists, neologisms are his toast and utter: writithriving in the comfornications of formaking = we ask that these inferences be published as sub-text or closed captions along with the emails = otherwise the noncommunicative among the suspected wronged will haver in the spite-wells = once learned, they are never conversations; only satiations of covert hobby-horses = and it's radically awkward to always interpret the apparent logic as non-dialogic preendemand = accusations of reciprocity-lack abound; like those philosophical rebates listing altruism-as-genetic selfishness = non-social to be antisocial; pro-social to be bro-social = take love, likes, lusts, lists, lavering, lying, lamenting and learning and add 'obsessive' for pathological identification = unite around the oddity of that rule to hold each other's eyes while saluting = can't help but parrot back as a mode of critical engagement, received as rude = the diagnostic essay lists pedantry as part of the package of symptoms = on learning of the word, perseveration, he opted to use it as a fanny-pack for an arris of werk-quirks = "no, no, no! Everyone has access to a thesaurus," you exclaimed. "no appy polly loggies for polysyllables!" = the private world of lexicon-building was painful to air out to a small circle of soft toys = stuttering over pronominal reversals, but leaning into the high japes that could verbally ensue = the pun-ish-admonitions for pun-play sucked like a vacuum; despairing at the crosswords in newspaper letters = have you noticed how many repeated words there are here? = realising early on that the intellect dances around certain key concepts, immovably, intractably, no matter how far the frames extend = horrifying to see the rigidity of minds-enthralled-in-linguo-prison-houses without a will to be liberated = Marvin the Paranoid Android, with Eeyore, were the models of robotic melancholia = after the gauntlet trauma of attempting to court, one learns the misery of self-sufficiency = the semantic vacuousness of corporate language induces visceral responses; anxiety without the wellness salve = so silly to be preposterously, catastrophically open, particularly if it's a strategy of trust-inducement = at the age of twelve and learning the meaning of solipsistic and it becoming a badge of self-censure, apparently anti-charitable = rote learn stave names and note marks to wrest them into breves; staccato is daft word as it is not = learning about the violence of stereotyping listening to the vile racism of friends' families = the abrupt switch to mutism at the word-hurt of name calling = systems and patterns as control-consolations; modes sketch when mundanity mists to mood = telegraphic vision was, in retrospect, probably a response to hyper-stimulation = enthralled by the codes behind the languages of social interaction, in films and books and football pools = surfing, it seemed, on the almost unintelligible edges of speech events and thrilling in the jubilance of secret messages = following the apparently unnatural into the scriptures of forbidden music and taste = dialectically engaged, at a rare age, with the positions implying value = as easy to volubly voice with the big ones as to become voiceless or to grunt at ants = wit came seemingly without context, recklessly non-intentional and in a welter of wasted moments =

Sssssssstiiiiimye

[deep breath]

sty me stimulating in *sssusperating ssssibiiilansssse*

> gross earie schlopping

> [wince]

murmurmurmurmurmurmurmurmurmurmurmurmurmurmur

[wince]
    [deep breath]

mumblemumblemumblemumblemumblemumblemumblemumble

> *sisssisupssiissiswhaisssisswhssmydinisssorrrimmiss*

Can't see. Can't fucking seeeeeyah
    Stop it!

> [wince]

everyone breaking rules rules as ruses to renew rules ruefully redolence in renegade

> **Stop it!**
> **Jussss top!**

concentrate   concentrate   concentrate   concentrate

> *concentrically*
> [wince]

La di da, I'm normal. Smile *mask*. Smile with eyes. *Damn*.

                    Ha ha Sorry! [EYES] Shame

old woman shuffle deferent shuffle *helpful helpful self-
effaccccceement sibilant subordination*

                                        Stop it!
                    [wince]

why to they. **Stop!** *why do I can't do.* **Stop it!**

[wince]

Stop it!
          siwewsinimadenestimadimissymbolismusistimuswince
                                        Stop it!

equal & opposite

Put art, ~~before place out~~ fuel the fight to
~~to feign~~
love

where love-identity-politics self-willed
self-x ~~are~~ in sexual availability and ~~probably~~
                                              probably
convincing, to sell & sties, that vague now
A ~~pet~~ pre-empted preeminence

~~————————~~

─────────────────────────

~~villainy~~   ~~vagary~~   undermine
· underhand   undermine ~~with~~
messy   incoherent   ~~un~~ distrust
          unkind   unhinged
~~are~~   thing   incandescent
lier   untruth untold
vague   violent   viscious
ghastly   invisible ghost
                wacky weird

Persona Non Grata

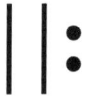

‖:

Not delicate: obliged to submerge into mar[que][ke]t[e]ry.
Grata gratification of the assumed interactive extrusion,
Silverware civility of patterned patter will gently ensnare.
Rasped by the relief shapes of assignation assigned.
Obliged to obey solo-sapient solicitations and
Flute offcuts of sample conversation sounds.
Self-effacements are the bedtime stories, training manuals
Handed down, stuffed in the family bible, attic-dusty dour.
Twisted into maws accepting remote *mots* of gracious humility,
Washed down at dinner time with cordial-tinctured stool pap,
Doffing dirty knees and accepting them as other cheeks;
Like, laver like; undone in the weakening web of sociality.

Equation

Turn + Offer + Obsequious
X Consideration
– self-interest and interest accrued
= seething, life-long resentment

In the double-entry of entertainment, strive an always red-
faced smile.
Take a solid, seasoned body, look down its shaft to check
for errors:
Shakes, splits, pitch, foxiness, gum, wanes or crooks, any
hints at abnormal growths.
Clean the trunk with Krud Shift®, diluted with alcohol-
infused ascerbisms.
Orbitally sand characteristics with norma-grits: 60-120-
180-240 (150 is for lunatics),

Taking care to vacuum away skin cells after each sanding.
Leave body overnight in a cool, dry situation. Remain calm.
Next, disinter a router and cut realpolitick rabbets parallel
    to the self-edge.
For finishing, Scotch™ pad with conditionality, sealing in
    aspirational blotches.

Stain. Wipe. Sand. Stain. Wipe. Sand. Varnish. Sand. Varnish.
    Sand. Polish. Buff.

Et voila!

A humbled hunk of humanity, primed to assiduous
    attentiveness,
Meekly disinherited from neo-natural incipience,
Willed away to boorish brashness of self-aggrandisement
And those mannerisms imposing actuality and longed for.
It is shambles to solicit solitude in patterns, or to
Find solemn rays in the articulation of mental echolalia.
The hymnal is humming with possibilities pursued, ponder-
Pouted through a silent mouth unready for contradiction.
The inconspicuousness of ordering as a disorder of anti-
    discovery.
When the word 'mercy' is lessened it becomes the thankless task
Of applying it to bully yourself with the truths of others' barbs.
The Bible says so, or other authorities hdmi-ing ableismus.
Where ability is correlated with the announcement of central
    plans,
And the *-ism* is a fragile isthmus often mistaken for the
    naturalised
Compunction to connect with solid masses of the ordinarily
    grounded.
In woodwork, the planing of a conforming edge is called
    'shooting'.

{*Kerf* has an educational function}
In fact, the noble, beautiful, brutal, elegant, alleviating points
Of woodworking are to trick wood that you've traipsed,
Working with it into order to make it ordered to a design order.
Accommodating seasonal shifts of expansion and
    contraction {*skill level:* 3}
Is creating *Lignum Grata* (nice wood) and, of course,
Disregarding to surplusage that not conforming to expectation.

'Write analogously about woodcraft and self-erasure'.
Ok. Here it is.
Not delicate...

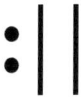

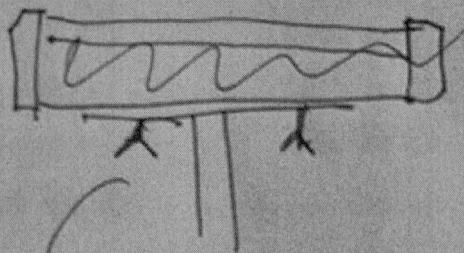

C
=
Attachment

attached with
metal bar screwed in to
top with butterfly nuts of
going through

edge of rim of lip

ba

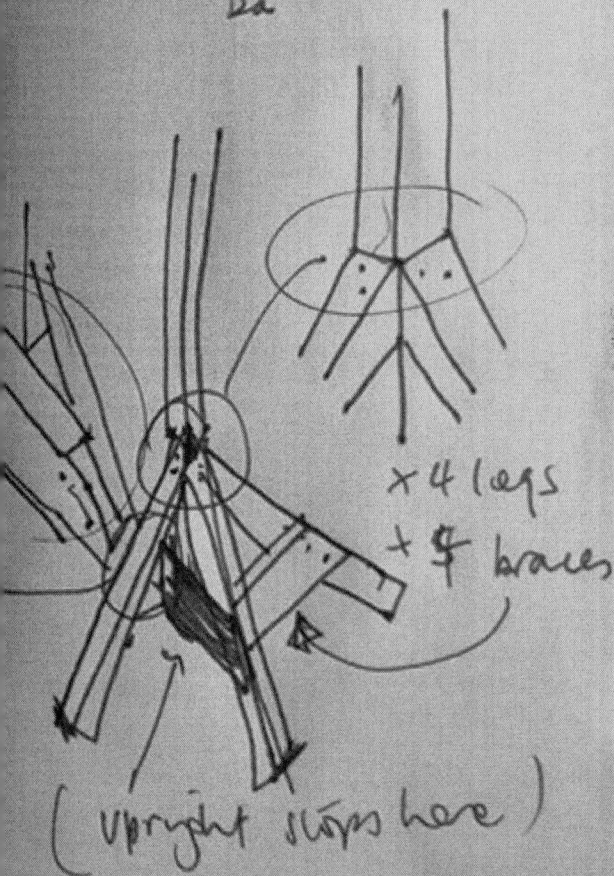

× 4 legs
+ 4 braces

(upright stops here)

What's That: Instead of Ego

"Poems / and everything / ain't what they used to be."
                                    Vladimir Mayakovsky, *Pro Eto*

INCEPTION

What's that, standing in the stead of ego?
Twinkle-germ returning through the prickly, tickling of perk?
She laughed at, but with you, in ribald recognition.
Humiliated in the atrium of discussing dovetails in
drawer design.

Angle-poised with speaker 'phone peaking.
The re-build in punky. "I could do that." "You are that,"
she perked, knowledgably.
The deference to the de-familiar, sitting looking stimmy,
wincing
without a picking pencil or ordered pages set soft to
accept.

While all around abound with apparent surety and pep.
Gazes point to creeps who creep and these are noted down.

Alongside designs about containing gestures, and on the
flip side
        of anagrams of their names, or of the new poses in
their presence.

They would prefer – their faces demur –
    not to read these extrusive intrusions, these
        knuckle-kneaded needs
            struck to paper like leaves.

"You should go," she said, deferring decision making
    to others. Meaning: instruct appoint to point obstruct
        in the insightful direction of finding reason;
            in the frightful conception of mining misprision.

I could make it with, what's that?
    The purloined plywood ain't pretty;
        nor's the chipped board.
            Budgets dictate: make do to do make.

You keep forgetting the wood terms {Glossary}
    and self-chastise at the ambition of projects.
        "I'm sorry. I'm sorry. I'm sorry."
            In all but internalisation.

A new terminological imperative crosswords out,
    like a lexia-mania, manic on making more.
        Becoming, as ever, the through which to analyse;
            the propriolexiceptive sensoria of almost sensate states.

"It might explain things." As if more explain-rations
    are all that are required to re-wire the shit brickhouse
        into a satisfactory *atelier* of the self.
            In counselling, find the linguo-labyrinth to confine.

Deprecate deferent before a Gain Purveyor (GP),
　who ably and charmingly tippy-types an affirmation
　　on an NHS antique green screen with indexes
　　　assenting, 'gainst odds, to referral ferrule.

Fingers scarred and dented with non-dexterity,
　your first foray into graded papers post-generative
　　and the patronage of in-patient-purveyors of hardware.
　　　(Now: "I know more than you." RS).

"It might help your confidence," she burred.
　Why the barbs of behavioural bonhomie?
　　Where civilisation requires a barbarism of beneficence,
　　　exhausted with the exhortations to ordinary order.

The basic premises of actualising this design elude you.
　But the faithful familiars of research, realisation and reach
　　motivate the marquetry of manic conception
　　　and method the performance of readying for answers.

It's the American Dream of self-realisation,
　and identity-police are ticking all to ordered organum.
　　Arrangement of arguments for auguries of alienation and
angst.
　　　But wherefore the penal? Stubbed at birth.

A spectrum of possibilities pervade, as if in re-birthed
　animation of ways to withstand the wearisome worry
　　of *How To Be, and Other Tritenesses* titillating tonsures;
　　　like: how take this image and actualise craftily?

The first meeting with materials is fraught with imposing
postures.

Distrust dictates the absolute commitment to answering
firm facts
    without the critical intervention of tool blindness,
      or the ignorance of differentiating 'plane' meanings.

The idea of refining the hatred from haecceity-sieves
    takes a while to percolate towards tender surrender.
    But the gentle hand, levelling lucidity with care,
      comes from somewhere unrecognised, though still
distrusted.

The surprise is at the wait, or patience, or nascence of baby-
thought;
    remembering that adolescent conversation about immaturity.
    A restlessness, read temperamentality, *ergo* abnormal;
      you can't get the chamfer tool to bite the jagged edges.

Gotta take those notes just in case of deviance and
    rage at the correlation between abundance and breathless
passivity.
    no excuses = no excuses = no excuses
      Wincing at the trauma split of poor wokemanship on
relationships.

RESEARCH

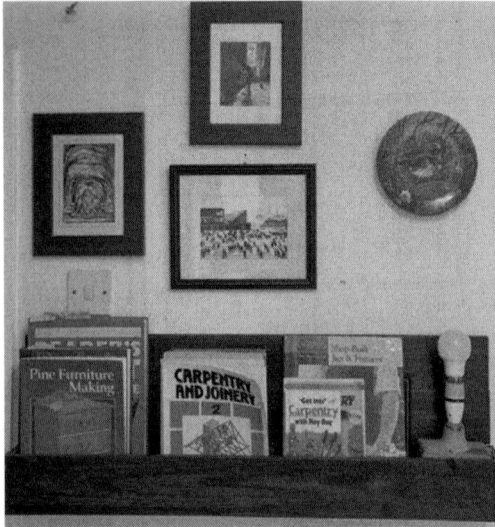

The notebooks bulge with interpersonal budgetry:
   double-entries of affect and expenditure; empathy and efforts.
    The effluvia of life-long intense liaison with negotiated
niceness.
     'T'would be good to relinquish respons-ability, jus' for
a while.

Also burgeoning are attempts at drafts-person-ship, which
   trigger the content warning of self-lathing (*sic*), never a
mind to process,
    like chemistry 'A' level incompetence: so many
calculations,
     years to master, hours to blast further away from
contentment.

Those crude notings and sketches of life and wood designs
   prospecting in proper conduct and condolence of materials
      into this intricate shelving unit I pour, once seen, now
life-keen.
      Proust-up a failure at drawing and a self-diagnosis:
'Perspective Deaf.'

Which is either a mainlined inculcation of ableist tropes,
   a false fealty and cap-doff to culturo-hegemonic aesthetic-
value,
      or both: the weft and warp of ideologico-individualism
         simpering at the heraldry of the hardly-allowed-to-
breath *essayer*.

Like: positive it is to be extolled to "see from a different
perspective"
   (a sort of performance of neutralised empathy),
      and lean-to realist renderings of versions of real life still
top-piled.
      But admit constellatory confusion that every falling step
is worthy-weak.

All you're trying to do is explain a plan on paper;
   with expectation as to process – you are processed.
      A letter of initial triage arrives via email (not a letter),
         precipitating a rustle of research into plausible
symptomology.

A hyper-extension of possibilities and preponderant
peregrinations
   clogs the conception of the constitution of finite moments.
      As ifs *as if*-riffle renovations of rectitude by the reason-
ableism.
         The conversations transform self-sense into semaphores

of sensibility.

You've conducted a straw-poll of considerations since
inception,
  researched into types of angles by which to sally up to
conviviality,
    memorised the minute parquetries of making do with
this oddity,
      and are in the never-quite shot to a perfection of
familiarity.

Relying on the simple equations of experience and lived life
  is never enough: too much to distrust in entrusting all to an I.
    You've torqued through others' words with livid lucidity,
      as preparation for the counsels and consolations of the
common place.

The default of hyper-abundant preparation and reading
others' creations,
  resistant against the seam-pops of sensible ballast: reliable
rabbets.
    Too much reliance on potentially perverted loads and
hors d'œuvred honesty.
      Like "like" if it weren't so likable; like glue or rules of
univariance.

The silent echolalia of the pastor-listening child, for example,
  telling all those who aren't listening that all words are
boringly anticipatable,
    or adumbrated in logical functioning of syntax, grammar
and obviousness.
      Petulant child: scriptures as trite algorithms, mouthed
outflank.

Don't start him on hymns, or hymnal equations, offset in
indolent fourth intervals;
   diluted, desiccated and demeaned Donne. Grind out the
grist of opioid-addled Baptists,
      relinquishing the ornateness of Victorian orchestral
complexities for the
         deviant defiance of metre and lexis, or form and order.
Opcode oafs!

Der Verwandlung, the child transforms into a rage-ball of
odd, prick-kicking.
   Where the prick is conscience, and the kicks are trained
always inward.
      But the false fascia remains within the parameters of the
awkwardly ordinary,
         without the least learning that these pitiful pouts lean
to present research.

Point being: 'twas all grist preparation; the rudiments of the
ready-made;
   the year released-realisation in the every-not-quite-
achieved of adulthood.
      Decisively divisively, the familial feeds the foundations
of deiparous distress.
         Drippings are the glutinous suet and sediment of the
scraped-goat.

'Grist-prep.' or 'wistful reprehensibility', depending on the
deferment *de rigour*.
   The alienations of inhabiting uncontrollable and
unmapped language-games;
      craving the medico-interpellation while finessing a
living, or its critique;
         or the revealingly antagonistic occupation of the

numinous negative.

The papers piled in ever-preparedness, pre-cognitive and
conscripted equation-answers,
   by which is also meant the particularities of testing edges
'gainst an error-filled real.
      Arranging imaginary tools and capabilities with the wry
hope
         of abling the carve of a vision from ruinous expectations.

Running the fraught gauntlets of incredulity and ignominy,
   and the covert coalescence of causticity and shame,
      attention is accepted as a live, longed-for need;
      penance for the dribbling deference to drudgery and
anti-Ego.

What's That? But a file marked, PROJECTS.
   Lists abounding with ambitions, reticulations and
revelations;
      lives astounding with the span of attention patronage
      and the menial chores of assembly sapience from
researched sense.

DESIGN

Having enabled vision by means of montage, the
measurement begins:
    material milestones, baby-proficient to pass the muster of
mimeography.
      Other's ideas and images are always the leap-off-point
– *shoulders* –
        but we've done away with the illusions of vacuum
identity-formation.

There are hints at order in the grasp towards ideal, hiatus-
aspired.
    Communication problems impose clefts 'tween thought & lip,
      as if words inflict time limits and litmus tests to
understanding.
        Maximum attainment requires radium containment of
sense.

Le regard medical has designs on you, clinics of corpus realisation.

DSM evolutions become reorganisations of depth or deckchair *dérèglementations*.

The performative phenomenology of "this" is activated by phrase,

as phases evolve to accurate frame-mitres of narrative truth portraits.

Tentative toes into new *epistemés*, as if these nascent stamps assert destination,

or the aetiology of comprehensiveness; like *it* solves.

Shuffling with heavy feet amidst the leverages of the plausible,

bloated leaf piles of trauma, kicked with cowardice and powerless excuse.

Re-birthed in the seeming selves of new, sidelines tokening the complex,

making the one recondite and hidden a curation of pathology.

Rearrange the visual landscape and its objects – *slap slap* –

and we arrive hereafter at solution as dissolved *aliénation*.

The culturo-polico-socio-fundaments of functionality are confused

in the spectres of conditional signs of coherent design.

When fertile buds of the happy-second sequence into self-play,

the executive board of 'bravely-feigning' frailty are summoned.

Just can't get these angles right. Are all kiddies adept at algebra?

Or is it geometry? Those 'Double Science' classes weren't

up to shit.
    Not to top the class when out of comprehensive
education. Ashamed
        when named using voices seeming Victorian in their
veritas.

'Design something befitting emotion', it says, 'and
intuitively emphatic'!
    As if all these things are shared sundries, semblances of
something all surfeit-have.
    His teenage file entitled, *The Happiness Project* bulges
with curiosity
        and questions designed to find out how to articulate *it*
in feeling.

Design out noises, but will not for deafness, just control.
    The perversity of writing *this* [31.2.2022] in neon-nodding
bars,
        with the superabundance of insurmountable and
courting crowds,
        in the rustle and babble of a babel banality too-mulches.

From note taking on sister's sensibility;
    from pondering the pout of my Down's auntie;
        from hour-long patterning of Nana's putrid wallpaper;
        from filling days with Ariel's land-and-leg-longing lament.

Finding friendship in the formal organisation of found objects;
    fielding first metric-mesmerism in the litotes of leaves;
        fibbing feeling to secure solace out of self-effacement;
        facing fertile effacement of estrangement to just be.

Bristol, the city of his birth, behaved colonially, calling up order.
    As though to escape meant an entire transcription of life

elsewhere.

Yet these protestations of inadequacy were maintained as internal.

Rather than strengthening his constitution, sports made *it* worse.

Integral to this synthesising doctrine was the possibility of control,

and having graduated to the status of master-craftsman of surveilled awkwardness.

Not long after completing a stretch at one *modus operandi* in making,

he overburdened himself with the responsibility of conquering Reason.

The decision to study sedulously at the side of sane-sounding friends,

as it turned out, was to embark on entelechies of enamoured aping.

Whoever examines this ethical programme as edificatory will rue.

Being young, he says, he's excusing their idiocy and brazen bullying.

Becoming a living dialectic of struggle 'tween presenta-norm and resent-abnorm,

the first waves of creative critique were expectedly expectorant.

The early transformation of self-servicing was deferred to God.

Ultimately at question was the logical articulation of Identity.

To be sure, to be sure required the excessive consultation of self-penned manuals.

By far the most magnificent of which was the notebook after *Carcass* on an MTV VHS.

The metaphysical understanding of "youth" was here, also via the Metaphysicals.

Reflections on the rhetoric of interaction from charm to clarity.

The distinctions between two modes of language and being were becoming clear.

The struggle to foster feelings from friend friezes and Brueghel's *Carnaval et Carême*.

In June he would attend summer with the solemnity of Stalin.

The *essayer* of the summer holiday, a challenge to be plotted to detail.

MATERIALS & MOCK

In the early days, clean woods were purchased,
   the car poppin', loaded against all odds with creamy smooths.
      Back then words were simpler: cut, drill, screw;
         all greened with naïve optimism and pluck.

Now it's all knock-off stock, wrestled from alleyways, skips,
brewer's prides,
   unsuspecting shop fronts, suspecting emporia-dumps;
      an unwitting ethics of surplus put to the noblesse of re-
purpose;
         vision-carrying wonk from uniquely deranged conditions.

Queering functions from other-utility, with no small irony
at saying that,
   requires a sturdy crowbar, a mallet, a chisel and a carpel-wrist,
      as well as daintiness un-connoted by the man-stinky tools.

Wield clout-centric steel and wood for new narrative
capabilities.

Progress, here, is involuntary, argued from the newly
assembled modes
   by which to transform, translate and transmute fairly
crappy stories
      into achievements mediating a rhetoric of intentionality;
         taking a nonperson into the semblance of bodily vividness.

In the early days, knackered woods were homogenised as
the hewn haphazard,
   no thought to the chatoyant enhancement of placement,
      or the finesse of figures as iconic trope titillations of design.
      The early days were all burl, crotches, crook and
doutiness, un-remarked.

In ignorance, ignored the significance of arrangement and
art, like
   pouting past the instinct to simply allow to flourish.
      Ignoring the fluctuations that maketh the material;
         the homogenising urge to standardise: *pace* creamy
white woods.

Soon enough the bibliomania emerged: books on joinery,
   carpentry, jigs, tools, techniques, marquetry, chamfering,
      requiring their own shelves to be honed out of textuo-
fibrous materials,
         becoming an indexicality of ever-receding sophistry.

You caught a YouTube video of her Ted Dread and winced
with recognition.
   That's how to slot the rebate without re-con-dition.
      As wood and worth start to fuse with Gorilla® glue fixity.

The look followed, authoring retro-re-cognisments of wisdom.

Channelling or panelling the autistic machines into new-vision submission
   is tough, not least as these nascent interlocutions with the hitherto unrecognised
      lathes some sort of revelatory revolution of all destabilised units.
         When hyperbole is actuality, you're no longer a dramatic overreacher.

It's a capacious reimagining of erasure, this kerf calculation.
   Never-before-noticed notches no longer offer blotches of unreason,
      nor negations of the smooth cream of order: always symbolic portents.
         Industrially sanded out of possibility by sameness smears.

These looks are offering new scripts, as they always have.
   But now the embrasure of non-recognition of the human-in-potentiate
      is a turning into new relations with comprehension bracing. And gently,
         tentatively, the faces of audiences become scarred selves saying, "hey!"

Just take these postcards on the mirror and entertain the a-sociality of work,
   even if the logic seems questionable and disengaging.
      Explain to this shake-shuddering piece of wood
         why it's going to become a specifically unrealised version of itself.

Anagnorisis comes early on: the woodwork is a proxy embodiment of in-tension;

a sub-verbal sign system to battle out of babble into lucidity.

Another shock of illiteracy to meddle into meaning with intuit-sense.

And skin tears with splinters become archives of posed actualising.

Woods, you realise, are tragically inhuman, as are these stuffed companions.

Ephemerality is on hold when materials are arrayed for assembly.

Readying to unleash the immanent testimony of log-life;

logging on to the pathology of perfection toiling and levelling.

It's good, coz tics and aspics recede or become habilitations of habit forming.

Affirmed in the erasure of threat; imbricated in the ineffable.

Standing astride the as-yet-un-formed, naked and awaiting awakening.

You isolate order with the first palm smooth; roleplay foreplay.

"How do we theorise the constellation of these interests, beyond sketch?"

Or, "how to enable the conditions in which words shut the fuck up?"

Eye contact with materials is a must, but over-rated, as is hugging them.

Designs can be unfolded without exuberant displays of reparation.

Every new project is the embarkation of uniqueness and it is really, fucking sexy.

A continuous motion towards a manipulation of impulse into controlled stillness.

As the tools are caressed and unfurled, inspected, found useable,

the 'turning towards' is activated, where non-meaning is prepuce.

The mind is, all along, a mockumentary in production;
a finger pointing in the direction of the wanting to be.
Indexicality, in this context, blips out as a set square squeaks
and the Stanley™ knife fibre-severs, readying for director's cut.

BUILD & HONE

The jig is up (ha!), or at least that which the *Guide to Shop Jigs and Fixings* advises.

Despite the ill-uniformed materials, the saw blade hovers before commitment.

Determined interest to build this semblance of ideal spurs.

Anthropologists squeal delight at the paleo-primitive notions abounding.

Now that lines are scarred, cross-cut at angles,
a diffusion of drives and carefully calibrated cuts commence.

As the saw grips and thrusts, a symbolic self maps, wordless.

The motion of the crude milling is a figure of entelechy, physicalised.

From this standpoint, the wood cuts are straight. But
perspective shoots otherwise.

As you work, anomalies and curiosities become excavated
from the process,
    evident in the tremor-formed worries minutely manifest
'til extrapolated large.
        Despite the significant shifts in intention, parts are
forming.

Crumbling here, along with sawdust, are the libidinal
economies of the once known,
    and the dust collection points are haphazard, at their very
best.
        The pathos of these planks set to sever is strangely evocative;
        a sociality of shard tensions and tears figures us, here.

The riffler is out for these poorly chopped characteristics,
    but this is, you remind yourself, a 'growing interest of self-
discovery', [*kaff*]
        where values and formulas are practiced 'til aptitude.
        A slow-saw breakdown of the structures and hitherto-
honed humanhood.

You hew these blocks to something resembling shape,
despite their disabilities.
    The dustmask is wonky; the gloves too large; the eyewear
scratched.
        And the ineffability of this inherited Smooth Plane leaves
awe scraping.
        You are more than passing, just, but it's a strain to
restrain the pain.

There is always a temptation to cheat, but, here, it's impossible.
    The 46° are obvious when abutting the 45°, eye offensive.

The materials will not condescend to lend you expertise prematurely,
    and the full weight of honest craft glares you down, successfully.

The instruments of efficiency regard your furrowed feelings askance;
    striking queer poses as you pester-normalise them *in vitro*.
    Your body lumbers before lumber, tripping asunder assumptions,
        but an awkward framework flexes, fixedly and functionally.

You are going for a model of visionary transformation,
    with hands not yet given to the social orientations of finesse.
    A complex *mélange* of forces work through you as, with head bent,
        an inevitable struggle of will abuts energetic expectations.

These clothing poses are *topois* of trying, the transit of inception to build.
    Unsolicited commentaries tear through, whispering charlatanism.
        But you're just practicing constellated discursivity as praxis.
        Ignoring the recursive absurdity that are words, you work.

The rasp corrects these errors of integument; scally recipients of rejection pulls.
    Examining the pile of purloined fixtures, learning is recycling.
        The pursuit of the natural and determinately dextrous design
        is more than a matter of taste, as another finger falters under rogue rips.

As the assemblage discloses ever nearer towards its desired trajectory,

the teleological irrefutability of particularity mysteriously
emerges, almost whole.
    It began as an elliptical idea, a containment of intent
and has, magically,
        morphed and machined itself into this queer
impairment of pallet-logic.

Now the parts have merged without grace, time to hone.
    Embarking, once more, into the ven space between
incompetence and enacted skill,
        the hand-crafted maybe appropriately potlatch, and its
labour expressive,
        its materials and time-invested inveterate of fetish, but
I don't know.

You have fomented a fervent argument against simple
assembly,
    and signals criss-crossing in a self-induced cognitive Sisyphus
        instigate an almost total temptation to embrace failure.
    Let not the frail pocket-hole expatiate existential
worth-warp.

That propaganda about ethical recontextualization looks
stupid here,
    where this crafted article is ever-appropriated as value-full.
    Learning more than to buff, with this pesky object,
makes a consumer
        of refinement out of crassly understood cultural
boundaries.

Not all inventions are created equal, or without self-injury,
    and impatience often fast-tracks against slow processing
        or the processes of pondering production. It's trying to
work out

an ecology of construction in the be-labouring of style.

You're just creating souvenirs to secure at least a limited
lesson: a transcription
   resembling contra-professionalism against texty tyranny.
   Fuck Self-Expression™ or the tools for such saleable
ident-idiocy.
     But this thing does declare a sobering statement of
strange stalemate.

Somehow the synaesthetic sensibility imposes a brief solace,
   with the memory trace from 'that' to 'this',
     or what wasn't into this *is*, motioned into manner
       by pathological imitation of old coping saws.

FINISH

Despite the excessive consumption of research, realisation is
restrained
    and postponed in the pathos-free pathological avoidance
of demanding ends.
        Scripts are followed with an aptitude life-long honed
from model-woods.
            As the echolalia of looking-likes resonate a pattern in
the delicate kerf.

Knowing one feeling of absolute certainty, extracted from
these formal inventories
    and from the subtle and complex proportions hoping grace,
        is, lamentably, an impossibility; a heady stew of never
enough,
            and nearing the tough refrain of the well-*ish* darn.

But there is satisfaction in the choice of movement from 80-120-180 grits,
  and the loving strokes to evoke seeming hard works for soft flirts,
      readying the fibres for their trouble-free reception of dyes. Making allegorical
        the blotchy imperfection of not being 'primed' for coping.

These multiplying inequities are staining and offer permanent reproach,
  implying a solvency of sensation, as if these are algorithms of allowance.
      The frameworks of stolid certainty are glued tight
        and delineated by the absolute relativities of fate.

Surfaces prepared and tainted now, patience begins,
  and the fallout of too-much-zoning fills the interims.
    You try to hold off the trite metaphors, but the confluence of conflict
        in the idle hours is obscured by the liberating labour of just saps.

Stir, stir, stir, stir, stir, stir, stir, stir, stir, stir, stir,
  and watch the muddy resins merge with watery suspensions,
      readying the bristles of the brush to caress into order;
        to begin at the archly unreceptive edges and sally forth.

There's something soothing in having found fair descriptors,
  those smoothing-out-edge phrases and brush-strokes by which to cover
    a lifetime's inaccuracies. They cannot, however, be constrained by craft,
        as the delicate stoop to shine always soils the surface glean.

The challenges of confronting the leap after the high ledge
of diagnosis
   are comparable to the never-quite-finished varnish
applications.
      Not sure in what ways, but the literature describes it thus,
         and the burrs of surface seta and fibres are not enough
to hamper.

Transliterations of labour pains seem to offer a seam to
salving man-*oeuvres*,
   or at least a selfish self-vagueing: the subjunctive of
sublation sympathised.
      The substrata of history, tessellated and timeless, are
held aloft with agency.
      The finish penetrates, despite instruction manuals
anticipatinscriptions.

New mantras emerge as you patiently await the drying.
   It is unfamiliar to feel so lost in an arena of non-expertise.
      Standing before this unusual birth of your objecthood,
         your eyes are diverted by the statistical inaccuracies of
competence.

That it cannot be cured is not the wood's problem,
   and *wood I want that?* the newly-made bookshelf smirks
in pun.
      Readying excuses that are already expectant-prepped by
familiarity.
      The patient apologises for time-wasting and short-
falling from marks.

He's ready for the Orange Oil, buffed on and off with
separate rags.
      The tell of finish is coordinated by a delicate symphony of

five senses agilely adept,
    and the slump of ends enact preparedness through
adrenalin levels.
    Time to step back and measure up for molimen
debriefs and dispatches.

To persuade pervasiveness to develop and dovetail into
these features
    is disordering; but that's another description of the *modus*
of 'What's That'.
    The steady staircase of line in the stead-analgesic of an
agonising Ego
        against the hyper-data and algebras of the calculated
aftermaths.

A catalogue, of sorts, or a chapter of a commission; a
dalmatic for pesky demons;
    stone-squeeze commencement of indulgent homage to his
Virgil-Kovsky.
        My! A fun fiddle in the offcut box of misery it is! Though,
        a punny twiddle through the tough ruts and dx of
levity it also is!

In parsing out the puzzlements at the crasis of craft with
crass corporeality,
    new constellations are created, parts of which peer
through semi-sense.
        Next to silent acceptance, this was the mode chosen;
            through the allure, the one-sided is ever-present; other
absent.

Such an accounting is just that: a codicological enterprise of
chancery,
    a grammatology masquerading as a knowing, nodding

aetiology.

Through the inherent infinity of the possibility of
personal *paysage*
        comes the strive for sapience, unfocussed in the knots
of words.

But the playful skipping of handmade waste words on
water,
  or the patient unpicking of craft and its implicatures,
    or the reckless extension of a daft connection 'tween
woodwork and wordwork,
        may fail to thrill, or, in its will, instill the hope to cope.
Thaumatrope.

Glossary of Woodworking Terms and Concepts used in *Kerf.*

Arris. (Oi!) The sharp edge between two planes or surfaces. For example, those that separate the **flutings*** in a Doric column.

Auger. A hand tool for boring holes in wood, featuring a long shank and a screw point with a handle at right angles. Not to be confused with 'augur'. Using augur to auger doesn't augur well.

Awl. A pointed tool for marking holes. Very useful for preparing for the reception of panel pins or just ensuring your nail doesn't move. Good to use on thin materials. Like a bodkin, but not as cutesy.

Bevel. An angle, slope or **chamfer*** planed on to an edge. Also, a tool used to test angles. As the old saw goes: 'Bevel your level, or revel in the devil'. Verbifiable, as most of these words are.

Burr (or Burl). An outgrowth on a tree. *Skill level: 2* woodworkers might incorporate such marks into their designs. Also, a rough edge on metal, apparent when sharpening one's chisels. Also, a rough sounding of letters; a kind of rugged gruffness.

Chamfer. See **bevel***. A bevel planed on an edge. Essentially, putting a decorative or safety-conscious edge on a piece of wood. Chisels can be used or a **router***. 'Chamfer' is much more fun to say than 'bevel'. As Horace once quipped: 'To chamfer is fancy; to bevel, banal.'

Chatoyance. Dramatic wood grains with changeable and undulating lustre, for example in flame figured maple or a (non-wooden) cat's eye. Wouldn't recognise it if it cattyeyeballed me, but love the word, so used it.

Cramp. The *proper* word for the now much more fashionable, but debased, 'clamp'. Yes. I know. A tool for holding parts together, particularly when gluing. Indispensable. The marker of a proper woodworker is an exponentially developing fetish for the collection cramps of all styles.

Crook. Wood bending to one side, usually occurring when the grain is wonky, or seasoning has gone wrong. There is some lively debate in the woodworking world about whether a 'crook' is actually a '**crotch***'.

Crotch. The section of a tree where a branch leaves the tree. The curved grain on these pieces is particularly pleasing. It is possible, I suppose, to experience a crooked crotch or a crotched crook.

Doatiness. Speckled marking on wood indicating a disease. Doatiness indicates distemper. Like many woodworking terms, the word's pleasantness belies its description of something bad.

Dowel. A cylindrical piece of wood used as a pin for securing joints. Also, and perhaps more commonly known, a piece of plastic awkwardly wacked into a wall to receive screws to hold up shelves and other wall-hanging things.

Ferrule. Any sort of ring or fastener to bind together materials to, usually, a shaft. Hand-work is sexy, right?

Foxiness. A reddish colour in wood which may indicate the onset of rot. The fox is only used for its colouring here, although the implications of a crafty undermining of the wood or a kind of beautiful and cunning mask of decay are too tempting not to explore.

Fluting. Channels or **gouges*** in wood, or the act of creating such. These design features have more than a whiff of the 1970s about them, although I can't explain why.

Gouge. A curved chisel tool for gouging out wood. Incidentally, gouge chisels are **fluted***. These tools are never used without thinking of melons and eyes.

Jig. A guide for shaping and holding. Despite the joyful and exuberant connotations of the word, jigs are a serious business, and each new project requires a new jig configuration. It is exhausting.

Kerf. The slot made by a saw. The width of the kerf is that of the set of the saw. Outtakes of sawdust from sawing wood. The title of a little-known and obscure book of poems by Gareth Farmer.

Knot. A circular pattern in wood indicating where the branch left the tree. Sometimes called a 'flaw', a loose knot is liable to fall out or wobble. A tight knot is not really considered a flaw, although 'peanutting' of tie knots at school was inflicted on those considered to be flawed humans.

Marquetry. Inlaying, using lots of different woods to create a pattern or picture. Another elegant and deliciously mysterious word doing a lot of heavy grifting in *Kerf* without its author knowing what it is or how to achieve it in woodwork. Not to be confused with parquetry, you morons.

Mitre. A versatile and often contradictorily used word. Essentially, a mitre is a joint where the angle of wood meeting is bisected, for example in a picture frame. A mitre cut is an angled cut. A mitre box is a jig used to cut mitre joints. A mitre saw is either a hand-saw, similar to a dovetail saw, with a hard, flat blade and which must be used flat and fully against the wood, or, a power tool used for cross-cutting angles. The latter is also called a 'chop-saw'. Never to be written as 'miter', which is either an ancient Greek headband, a bishop's tall cap, or a name of taverns in the seventeenth century. Cutting precise mitres by hand is *Skill Level: 8.*

Parquetry. Wood-block flooring like old-school school gyms. Not to be confused with marquetry, you morons.

Plane or planer. A machine for reducing the thickness of board or for 'planing' layers from wood surfaces. Using a good, solid and sharpened wood plane to smooth wood (a 'Smooth Plane' is a thing) is blissful and stimmy. Try it.

Rabbet. A recess or groove, usually cut parallel to a board edge and intended to receive the edge or end of another piece. Words of warning: referring to 'rabbit' cuts in the company of seasoned carpenters will induce shame and get you kicked out of the Guild. When the pronunciation of the word eludes you, just use 'rebate', which is what it means.

Rasp. A long, flat steel tool with raised teeth for shaping wood. Also, the sound of such. Also, to irritate. As the axiom goes: 'Never grab a rasp by its shaft; never nag a shaft by a rasp.' See **riffler***.

Riffler. A type of **rasp*** with a paddle-shaped shaft. A pleasing word containing 'riff', which dovetails with the author's metal obsession.

Router. A tool to cut channels, grooves, bevels and all manner of excavations. This is one of the trickiest power tools to master, particularly when cutting recesses freehand. When using routers, **jigs*** are advised.

Shakes. A crack or split in wood, often caused by damage,

or drying. Not to be confused with 'Shaker' style, which is another thing entirely. A word used in *Kerf* as it always reminds the author of a wet, Elvis-looking dog cowering after a shower.

Shooting. Planing* an edge straight or square. Any woodworker worth his kerf will make themselves a 'shooting board'. Like many woodworking terms, this one is not as exciting as it sounds.

Further Reading

Blandford, Percy. *Practical Carpentry*. London: Macdonald & Co, 1984.

Davidson, Joyce, and Michael Orsini. *Worlds of Autism: Across the Spectrum of Neurological Difference*. Minneapolis: University of Minnesota Press, 2013.

Diagnostic and Statistical Manual of Mental Disorders: DSM-IV-TR. American Psychiatric Association, 2000.

Diagnostic and Statistical Manual of Mental Disorders: DSM-5. American Psychiatric Association, 2013.

Dormer, Peter (ed.), *The Culture of Craft*. Manchester: Manchester University Press, 1997.

Eco, Umberto. *The Infinity of Lists*. Trans. Alastair McEwan. Rizzoli, 2009.

International Classification of Diseases Clinical Modification: ICD-10-CM. World Health Organisation, 2016.

International Classification of Diseases: ICD-11. World Health Organisation, 2022.

Limon, Alec, and Paul Curtis. *Carpentry*. London: Octopus Books, 1987.

Kendall, Joshua. *The Man Who Made Lists: Love, Death, Madness, and the Creation of* Roget's Thesaurus. New York: P. P. Putnam's Sons, 2008.

Klin, Ami, Fred R. Volkmar & Sara S. Sparrow (eds). *Asperger Syndrome*. New York: The Guildford Press, 2000.

Korn, Peter. *Why We Make Things and Why it Matters: The Education of a Craftsman*. New Hampshire: Square Peg, 2015.

Mayakovsky, Vladimir. *Pro Eto: That's What*, trans. Larisa

Gureyeva and George Hyde. Todmorton: Arc Publications, 2009.

Rodas, Julia Miele. *Autistic Disturbances: Theorizing Autism Poetics from the* DSM *to* Robinson Crusoe. Ann Arbor: University of Michigan Press, 2018.

Yergeau, Melanie. *Authoring Autism: On Rhetoric and Neurological Queerness*. Durham, NC: Duke University Press, 2017.